D1023525

Think Like a Computer

by Marcie Flinchum Atkins

Content Consultant
Sarah Otts
Scratch Online Community Developer
MIT Media Lab, Massachusetts Institute of Technology

Reading Consultant
Jeanne M. Clidas, Ph.D.
Reading Specialist

Children's Press®
An Imprint of Scholastic Inc.

Library of Congress Cataloging-in-Publication Data
Names: Atkins, Marcie Flinchum, author.
Title: Think like a computer/by Marcie Flinchum Atkins.
Description: New York, NY: Children's Press, an Imprint of Scholastic Inc., [2019] |
Series: Rookie get ready to code | Includes bibliographical references and index.
Identifiers: LCCN 2018027253 | ISBN 9780531132258 (library binding: alk. paper) |
ISBN 9780531137000 (pbk. : alk. paper)
Subjects: LCSH: Computer science—Juvenile literature.
Classification: LCC QA76.23 .A86 2019 | DDC 004—dc23

Produced by Spooky Cheetah Press
Creative Direction: Judith E. Christ for Scholastic Inc.
Design: Anna Tunick Tabachnik

Published in 2019 by Children's Press, an imprint of Scholastic Inc.

Printed in North Mankato, MN, USA   113

SCHOLASTIC, CHILDREN'S PRESS, GET READY TO CODE™, and associated logos are trademarks and/or
registered trademarks of Scholastic Inc.

2 3 4 5 6 7 8 9 10 R 28 27 26 25 24 23 22 21 20 19

Scholastic Inc., 557 Broadway, New York, NY 10012.

Photographs © cover center: szefei/iStockphoto; cover and throughout robots: the8monkey/iStockphoto; cover
and back cover background: RioAbajoRio/Shutterstock; inside cover and throughout: pmmix/Shutterstock; 4
dashed line: Golden Shrimp/Shutterstock; 4 and throughout birds: Andegraund548/Dreamstime; 5 appliances:
primiaou/Shutterstock; 5 cars: FuzzyLogicKate/Shutterstock; 5 game controller: H Art/Shutterstock; 5 and
throughout cell phone: Astarina/Shutterstock; 7: ChickenDoodleDesigns/Shutterstock; 8: michaeljung/
Shutterstock; 9 printer: macrovector/iStockphoto; 11: NASA/Science Source/Getty Images; 13 top left: ICP/
age fotostock; 13 top right: vgajic/iStockphoto; 13 bottom left: metamorworks/iStockphoto; 13 bottom
right: dolphfyn/Shutterstock; 14-15 girl: Fortunato Photography; 14 sink: vitaliok01/Shutterstock; 17 mouse:
KsuperKsu/iStockphoto; 17 cheese: Mikhail Miroshnichenko/Dreamstime; 19: Alfmaler/Shutterstock; 20-21
girl: Fortunato Photography; 20 sink: vitaliok01/Shutterstock; 22: Bloomicon/Shutterstock; 25: early cell
phone: LockieCurrie/iStockphoto; 25 candlestick phone: Joey Swart/Dreamstime; 25: rotary, cordless,
smartphone: BackyardProduction/iStockphoto; 27: xefstock/iStockphoto; 29 cat: ksuper/
Shutterstock; 30 cat: ksuper/Shutterstock; 30 dog: Burlesck/Dreamstime.

TABLE OF CONTENTS

CHAPTER 1
What Is a Computer? 4

CHAPTER 2
Programming Computers........... 12

CHAPTER 3
Bugs and Viruses........................ 20

CHAPTER 4
The Future of Computers............ 24

Debugging Challenge..........................28
Write a Code 30
Glossary 31
Index 32
Facts for Now....................................32
About the Author................................32

What Is a Computer?

We use computers at school and at home. We use them to do homework and look up information. We use them to play games and watch videos. There are even computers inside things we use every day.

Look around your house. Which things have a computer inside?

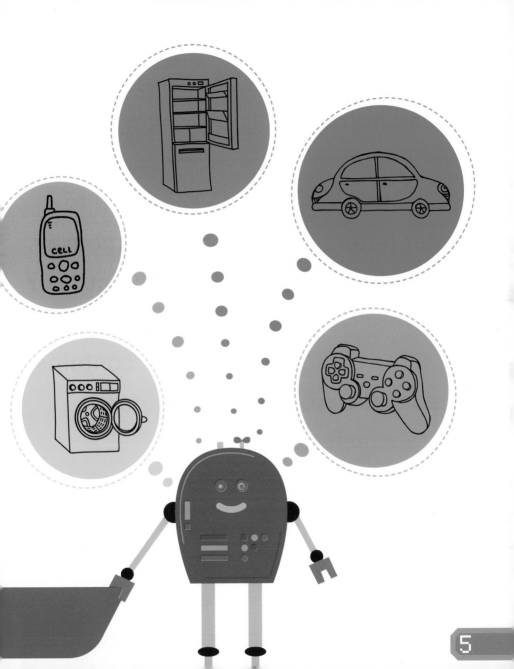

The different parts of a computer are called hardware. The monitor shows what you are typing or viewing on the computer. You use the keyboard to enter letters and numbers. A mouse or trackpad lets you move the **cursor** to different places on the monitor.
In some computers, a tower contains the hard drive of the computer.
It stores information.

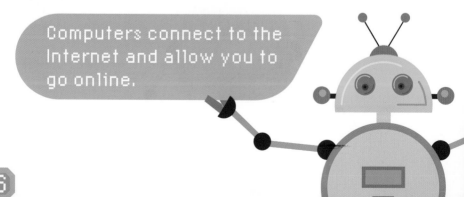

Computers connect to the Internet and allow you to go online.

Computer Hardware

monitor

tower

keyboard

mouse

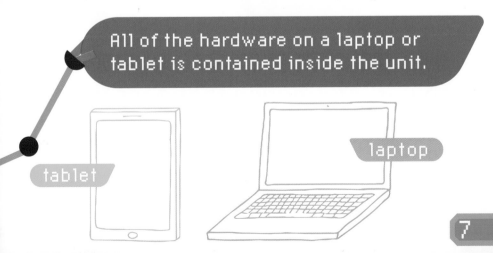

All of the hardware on a laptop or tablet is contained inside the unit.

tablet

laptop

Input is information that goes into a computer. Output is information that comes out of a computer.

When you type on your keyboard or tap a touchscreen with your finger, you are inputting information. The words you see on your monitor are output. So is a story that you print out from your printer.

output

Computers store files. They store words, pictures, videos, and games. Storage on a computer is measured in bits and bytes. Eight bits equals one byte.

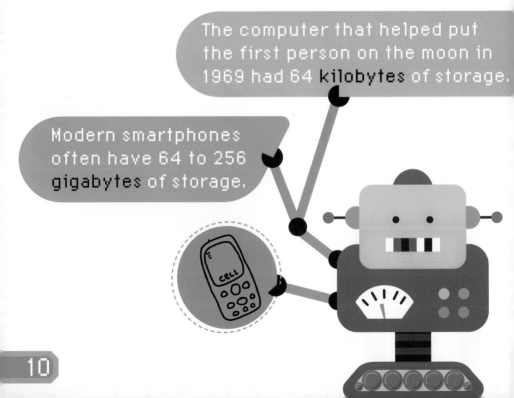

The computer that helped put the first person on the moon in 1969 had 64 kilobytes of storage.

Modern smartphones often have 64 to 256 gigabytes of storage.

1,000
bytes
=
1 kilobyte

1,000
kilobytes
=
1 megabyte

1,000
megabytes
=
1 gigabyte

1,000
gigabytes
=
1 terabyte

Chapter 2

Programming Computers

Computers cannot think or act on their own. They do what **programmers** tell them to do.

A programmer writes computer programs called software. We use software to write, do math, play games, and more.

write a program

play games

Software helps us
do all these things.

predict the weather

use maps

13

Algorithms are steps that are done in a certain order. Computer programmers use algorithms when they write software. You might be surprised to learn that we also use algorithms in real life!

Steps for Getting Ready for School

Wake up.　　Eat breakfast.　　Brush teeth.

You use algorithms throughout the day. Your morning algorithm might include eating breakfast, brushing your teeth, and getting dressed.

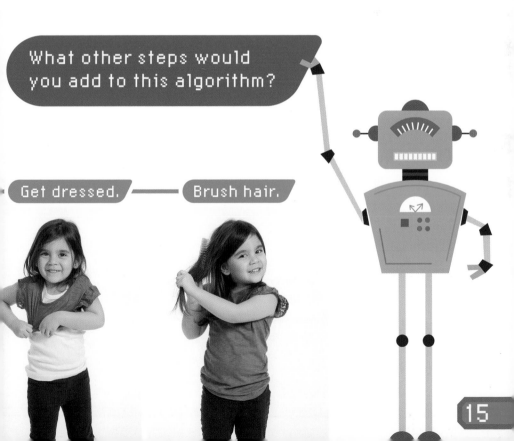

What other steps would you add to this algorithm?

Get dressed.

Brush hair.

Code is a language that a computer can understand. It is made up of words, numbers, and symbols. A programmer can change the order of the words, numbers, and symbols. That makes the computer do something different.

Coding includes a lot of algorithms.

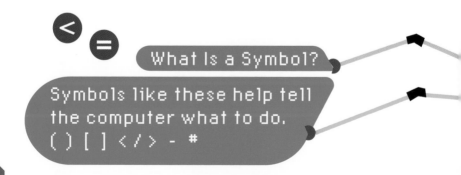

What Is a Symbol?

Symbols like these help tell the computer what to do.
( ) [ ] < / > - #

The mouse is hungry! This simple code will take him to the cheese.

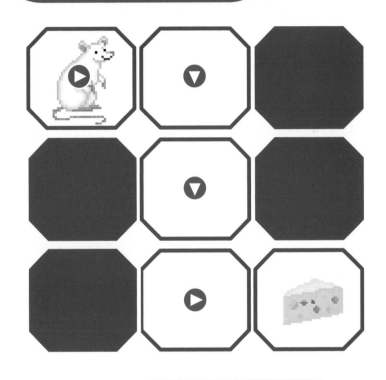

Coding Language

▶ Move one box right.
◀ Move one box left.
▲ Move one box up.
▼ Move one box down.

Often code repeats the same task over and over. That is called looping.

Think about when you stack chairs in your classroom. You stack each chair the same way. You might repeat the same steps 20 times.

Programmers do not want to enter the same line of code 10 or 100 times. Instead, they write looping into the code.

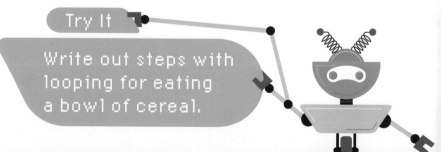

Try It

Write out steps with looping for eating a bowl of cereal.

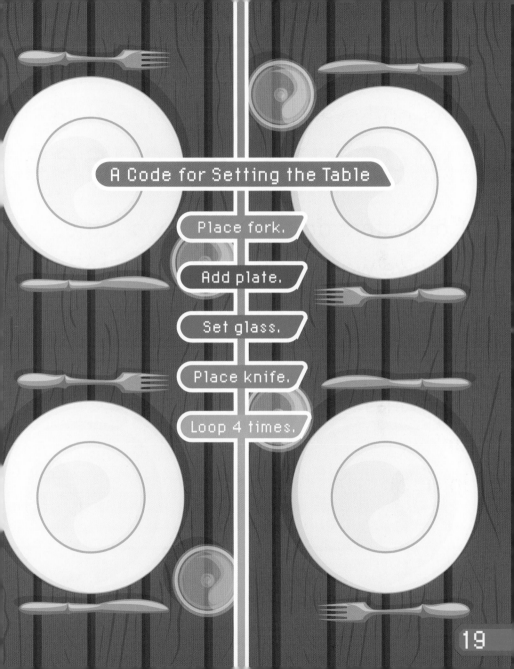

A Code for Setting the Table

Place fork.

Add plate.

Set glass.

Place knife.

Loop 4 times.

Chapter 3

Bugs and Viruses

Computers do not always work the way we want. A mistake in the code is called a bug. Programmers have to

Steps for Getting Ready for School

Wake up.

Brush teeth.

Eat breakfast

find the mistake. They have to fix it. That is called debugging.

Programmers go step-by-step through the code. They look for where it stopped working.

Where is the mistake in these steps?

Get dressed. — Brush hair.

A computer virus can make the computer stop working properly. It can make the computer crash. It can also steal personal information off the computer.

VIRUS ALERT

A virus can infect a computer through email, websites, or files. You can prevent viruses. Never download files from unfamiliar websites. Never click on files from people you do not know!

Don't worry: *You* cannot get sick from a computer virus!

Chapter 4

The Future of Computers

The world of computers is changing quickly. New **technology** makes computers better and faster.

You can do things with a computer that you could not do before.

You can even use a smartphone as a handheld computer!

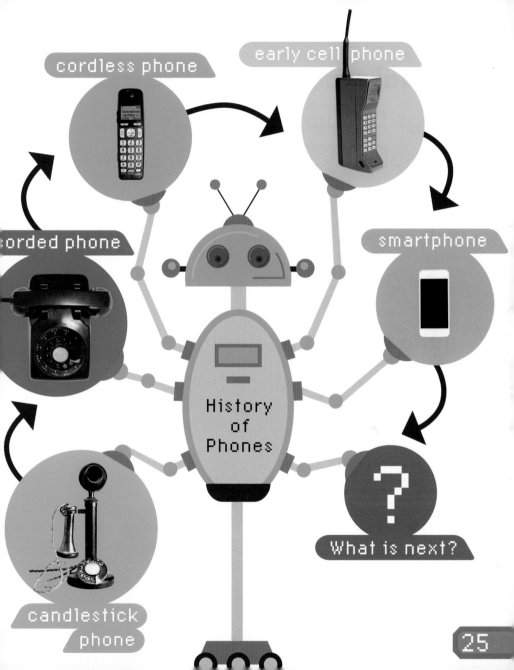

cordless phone

early cell phone

corded phone

smartphone

History
of
Phones

candlestick
phone

?

What is next?

Virtual reality lets you experience things through technology. For example, if you are interested in dinosaurs, you can use virtual reality to visit the Cretaceous period. If you want to be an astronaut, you can visit Mars.

In the future, you might not be able to tell the difference between what is real and what has been created with a computer!

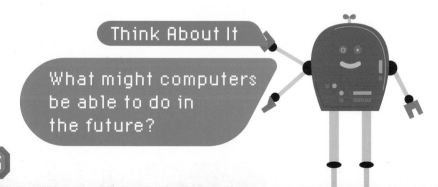

Think About It

What might computers be able to do in the future?

DEBUGGING CHALLENGE

Look at these signs and what they mean. This will be your code:

▶ Move one box right.
◀ Move one box left.
▲ Move one box up.
▼ Move one box down.

Now the cat is hungry!
The programmer has written the following code to get the cat to the mouse in the diagram: ▼ ▼ ▶
Spot the mistake in the code.
What should the steps be?

We filled in the first step.
What are the others?

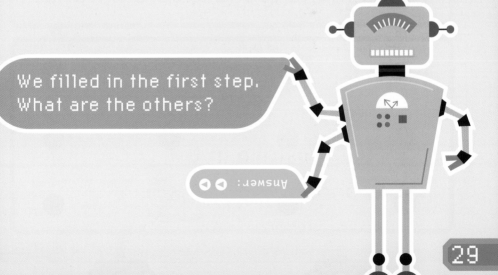

Answer: ◀ ◀

WRITE A CODE

Now this dog wants to play!
Use arrows to show the steps to get
the dog to the cat.

After you write a series of steps
using arrows, reread your code
with a friend to make sure it works.

GLOSSARY

algorithms (al-guh-**ri**-themz)
series of steps done in a certain order to do something useful

cursor (**kur**-sur)
flashing line, arrow, or other shape that shows your place on a computer screen

programmers (**proh**-gram-urz)
people who write programs for computers

technology (tek-**nah**-luh-jee)
use of science and engineering to make things easier

virtual reality (**vur**-choo-uhl ree-**al**-luh-tee)
environment that looks three-dimensional and real but is created by a computer

Think About It

Is there more than one code that can take the dog to the cat?

Answer: yes

31

INDEX

algorithms .. 14–15, 16

bugs 20–21

code 16, 18, 20, 21

hardware............6

input.............. 8, 9

looping............. 18

output.............8, 9

parts of a computer............6

printer 9

programmers 12, 14, 16, 18, 20, 21

software....... 12, 14

storage 10

technology.... 24, 26

virtual reality...... 26

virus 22–23

FACTS FOR NOW

Visit this Scholastic website for more information on computers: **www.factsfornow.scholastic.com**
Enter the keyword **Computers**

ABOUT THE AUTHOR

Marcie Flinchum Atkins teaches kids how to use computers and find the best books in her job as an elementary librarian. She holds an M.A. and an M.F.A. in children's literature and lives with her family in Virginia. Read more about Marcie at www.marcieatkins.com.